PARANORMAL SEEKERS™

TRACKING UFOS

JENNA VALE AND
JANET I. STIRLING

rosen publishing's rosen central
New York

Published in 2019 by The Rosen Publishing Group, Inc.
29 East 21st Street, New York, NY 10010

First Edition

Library of Congress Cataloging-in-Publication Data

Names: Vale, Jenna, author. | Stirling, Janet, author.
Title: Tracking UFOs / Jenna Vale and Janet I. Stirling.
Description: First edition. | New York : Rosen Publishing, 2019. | Series: Paranormal seekers | Includes bibliographical references and index. | Audience: Grades 5–8.
Identifiers: LCCN 2018016176| ISBN 9781508185765 (library bound) | ISBN 9781508185789 (pbk.)
Subjects: LCSH: Unidentified flying objects—Sightings and encounters—Juvenile literature.
Classification: LCC TL789.2 .V353 2019 | DDC 001.942—dc23
LC record available at https://lccn.loc.gov/2018016176

Manufactured in the United States of America

CONTENTS

INTRODUCTION 4

CHAPTER ONE
EYES TO THE SKIES 7

CHAPTER TWO
CLASSIC CASES 17

CHAPTER THREE
WHEN WORLDS COLLIDE 27

CHAPTER FOUR
DISTINCTLY STRANGE SETTINGS 37

CHAPTER FIVE
UFOS IN POP CULTURE AND BEYOND 46

GLOSSARY 54
FOR MORE INFORMATION 56
FOR FURTHER READING 59
BIBLIOGRAPHY 60
INDEX 62

INTRODUCTION

As part of the opening ceremony of the 2018 Winter Olympics in Pyeongchang, South Korea, 1,218 "Shooting Star" drones took to the sky in synchronized flight. An animator had predetermined the path, and the drones looked like living stars as they arranged themselves into shapes such as the Olympic rings and even that of a moving snowboarder. At the time, it was the largest group of drones to be used in such a way, and it took viewers' breaths away as they watched on their preferred screens across the world.

The drones made a phenomenal spectacle, even with viewers knowing exactly what these mobile lights in the sky were. As extraordinary as the drones were, how incredible must it be to witness strange objects in the sky and have no idea what they are?

Enter unidentified flying objects, or UFOs. In truth, UFOs could be so many things, from military aircraft, to tricks of the light, to weather phenomena. The strongest connotation, however, is that of flying saucers piloted by extraterrestrials. People associate UFOs with alien spaceships so readily that most other explanations end up sounding like efforts to cover up the truth. However, UFO sightings are perfect cases for testing one's reasoning skills. Approaching the matter scientifically will often lead to rational explanations. After all, the goal should be to identify the flying object, not jump to conclusions about alien visitors.

While humanity has gained much knowledge from studying the heavens for hundreds of years, there are still phenomena scientists have yet to understand, both in Earth's own skies and in the far reaches of space.

For example, on October 13, 2010, several New Yorkers stopped in their tracks when they witnessed "clusters of shiny round objects" floating over Manhattan. The sighting prompted several calls to 911; some people even claimed the objects seemed to light up and flash. Almost immediately, videos of the incident went up on the internet, prompting interest all over the world. However, the excitement died down pretty quickly when some students from nearby Westchester, who had been planning a big engagement party for their teacher admitted that some of their balloons had flown away and were likely the cause of the "sighting."

All of the attention those celebratory balloons received resulted in a speedy investigation and ordinary conclusion. Such cases are more common than people might think, but it's true that many UFOs remain unidentified, too. For hundreds of years, people have been trying to make sense of UFO sightings, and the possible explanations vary greatly. Furthermore, so many reported UFO sightings simply don't provide enough information to even narrow down what the flying object might be. Whatever is yet to be discovered, whether from this world or not, the history of UFO encounters is rich, puzzling, and sometimes unsettling.

CHAPTER ONE

EYES TO THE SKIES

It all starts with eyes raised to the skies above. People have always wondered what, if anything, exists beyond the clouds. Once humanity achieved the technological marvel of flight in the nineteenth century with airships, it was almost certain that people would begin to see manufactured objects in the sky that they had no frame of reference for. Meteorologists also began launching weather balloons near the end of the nineteenth century to study the atmosphere, further adding to traffic in the sky. The idea of man-made objects floating or flying in the sky must have seemed like the stuff of science fiction at the time, and indeed some stories made it seem that way.

THE UNKNOWN PILOT

On April 19, 1897, the *Dallas Morning News* published a report of an airship allegedly crashing in the town of Aurora in Wise County, Texas. According to the article, it collided with the tower of a windmill and exploded, scattering debris over several acres.

The press explained in the article: "The pilot of the ship is assumed to have been the only one aboard, and while his remains are badly disfigured, enough of the original has been picked up to show that he was not an inhabitant of this world." The article then goes on to give the time of the "pilot's" funeral. This incident was forgotten until the late 1960s, when an article in the *Flying Saucer Review* attracted investigators to Aurora. They found that no windmill had ever existed in the spot the article indicated and that there were no unmarked graves in the local cemetery.

In 1973, another article claimed that elderly citizens of the town remembered the crash and had even collected "unidentified" metal from it. It also claimed that

The supposed spaceship crash is even mentioned on the Texas Historical Commission marker at the Aurora Cemetery.

the UFO pilot's grave had been found through the use of a metal detector and that a "unique handmade headstone" was found on the spot. A court order was sought to exhume the "spaceman's" body.

Then, on July 4, 1973, the *Dallas Times Herald* carried the headline, "Grave Believed UFO Pilot's At Aurora, Entered, Robbed." Once again investigation proved that things were not as they seemed. The hand carved "tombstone" was a scarred rock, and the old-timers who had been interviewed all said they'd been misquoted and had never said they recalled the incident.

In the end, there was not one shred of evidence to back up the story of the Aurora crash.

WARTIME SIGHTINGS

Then, between 1909 and 1919, airships were seen over England. They were believed to be Germans, not aliens, scouting for an invasion. Reports of sightings also came in from Europe, the United States, Canada, Japan, New Zealand, and South Africa, possibly the result of nervousness about World War I.

From 1909 until his death in 1932, Charles Fort, a well-known writer who covered strange occurrences, reported numerous incidents of "unknown, luminous things" seen in the sky, many of them disc-shaped.

Then, just before and during World War II, there were reports of ghost planes in the skies over Europe. Allied pilots often reported seeing what they dubbed "Foo

Photos of Nazi flying discs were uncovered after World War II. The head of the US Air Force's Project Blue Book reported that most of the radical aircraft found were in early stages of development during the war.

Fighters" accompanying their flights. The objects were described as "large orange glows" or "small amber discs."

At first these were feared to be a Nazi secret weapon, but they appeared in the Pacific as well. None were reported to have directly interfered with Allied planes or crews—they simply flew quietly alongside them. After a while, less was heard of these objects, and eventually they became a spooky UFO story heard only occasionally.

RADIATION, OR SOMETHING ELSE?

On October 24, 1886, the nine members of a family in Maracaibo, Venezuela, were sound asleep when suddenly they were awakened by dazzling lights and a strange humming noise outside their house. Terrified, the people fell to their knees and began to pray, but this was soon interrupted by bouts of violent vomiting and swelling in the upper body, particularly around their faces and lips. The next morning, the lights were gone as was the swelling, but in its place the people found black blotches all over their bodies. Nine days later, the skin peeled away around the blotches and left red, raw sores in their place. The people began to lose their hair. Doctors found that the symptoms were very similar to those of radiation poisoning, but the house itself had suffered no damage, and throughout the event, none of the windows or doors had been open. It should also be noted that on the ninth day after the incident, all of the trees surrounding the house withered and died.

The story of the family appeared later that year in an article in *Scientific American*. In 2011, a reader discovered the original article and asked the editors at *Scientific American* about the story, prompting them to reexamine the incident. Editor Dan Schlenoff addresses the tale by admitting that there is not enough information to definitively say what happened

(continued on the next page)

(continued from the previous page)

to the family, but he also offers, "one of the prominent natural curiosities of Maracaibo is the Catatumbo Lightning—intense lightning storms lasting for hours and taking place during much of the year." Schlenoff goes on to say that the total effects of such lightning activity are not known. While what really happened to the Maracaibo family remains a mystery, the strange electrical energy of the area may be a piece of the puzzle.

MYSTERY ROCKETS

After World War II, beginning in May 1946, Sweden experienced sightings of spool-, torpedo-, or cigar-shaped rocketlike objects, often with small fins attached. At the time the fear was that German rocket technology was being used by the Soviets, and an extraterrestrial origin wasn't suspected. Between May and December, 997 sightings were reported. More than two hundred were of the "rocket-shaped" variety and were described as metallic.

Soon other nations began to make reports of "ghost rockets." France, Denmark, Norway, Spain, Greece, Morocco, Portugal, and Turkey viewed flashing lights in their skies, sometimes accompanied by "an infernal roaring." Eventually the Swedes were able to identify 80 percent of their sightings. The rest were listed as unidentified.

FLYING SAUCERS

In 1997, a top-secret report from 1948 was declassified. It confirmed that not all ghost rockets could be identified, and experts concluded that they could not rule out extraterrestrial origins.

On June 24, 1947, Kenneth Arnold, a successful businessman and private pilot, was on his way home and intended to make a detour to Yakima, Washington, to help search for a missing troop transport. It was about three o'clock in the afternoon; he was flying at 9,200 feet (2,804 meters), and the air was crystal clear—excellent flying weather. A flash of light off to the left caught his eye, and he looked toward Mount Rainier. He described what he saw as "a chain of nine peculiar looking aircraft flying from north to south at approximately 9,500 feet (2,896 m) elevation and going, seemingly, in a definite direction of about 170 degrees." Arnold estimated that they were between 20 and 25 miles (32–40 kilometers) away.

They were flying at a high rate of speed and were bobbing and weaving slightly, which caused them to flash in the sunlight. Arnold timed them as they passed Mount Rainier in the direction of Mount Adams. It took 102 seconds

Kenneth Arnold displays his own drawings of the crafts he saw. They were about 50 feet (15 m) long, but only 3 feet (1 m) thick. They had a mirror finish.

for the objects to pass between the two peaks. It is 47 miles (76 km) between Mounts Rainier and Adams, which gives the objects a ground speed of 1,700 miles per hour (2,735 km per hour). The speed of sound is approximately 740 mph (1,191 kph), making the mysterious objects capable of flying at over twice the speed of sound! In 1947, no aircraft on Earth had that capability.

Arnold took his maps and calculations to the local FBI office but found it closed. He then went to the *East Oregonian* newspaper and spoke to an editor there. The report that went out on the Associated Press wire said, "nine bright, saucer-like objects flying at 'incredible speed' at 10,000 feet (3,048 m) altitude were reported here today." Most researchers agree this is the report that coined the term "flying saucers."

After years of reflection, Kenneth Arnold noted that what had startled him most was that he had been unable to see any sign of a tail on any of the aircrafts he had witnessed that day. He speculated whether or not the tails had been camouflaged via some Air Force technology, but he honestly was never sure what the objects could have been.

THE EXETER INCIDENT

Air Force technology has been suspected as an explaination for UFOs in other cases, too. Very early in the morning on September 3, 1965, multiple people witnessed something eerie in Exeter, New Hampshire. A woman claimed that a UFO with flashing red lights had chased her off the road, and a police officer named Eugene Bertrand took her story down when he found her shaken by the roadside, but thought little of it.

A couple of hours later, around 2:30 a.m., an eighteen-year-old named Norman Muscarello rushed into the Exeter police station to report that something as big—or bigger—than a house with a group of five lights on it had appeared in the sky near where he had been hitchhiking along Route 150.

Officer Bertrand saw how unsettled Muscarello was and agreed to take him to the site to see if they could find out anything further. Just before 3 a.m., the pair arrived in the field where Muscarello had witnessed the object, and Bertrand, to his bewilderment, witnessed the very group of lights Muscarello had described. The lights appeared to flash and move in a distinct pattern, and in his shock, Bertrand fell to the ground and nearly drew his firearm because they seemed to come so close to them on the ground. Officer Bertrand radioed another patrolman, David Hunt, who joined them and also witnessed the phenomenon before the lights moved east toward the ocean and out of sight.

In the coming weeks, around sixty sightings of UFOs were reported in the Exeter area. The incident from September 3 had become widely publicized and no one could determine what the lights could have possibly been. Dr. J. Allen Hynek, the astronomer and ufologist who classified the five kinds of "close encounters" with UFOs, even commented that the Exeter incident was a good example of the first kind of close encounter: a UFO sighting within at least 150 yards (137 m).

So what had mysteriously flown and flashed over Exeter that September night? In 2011, a former military pilot named James McGaha and a ufologist named Joe Nickell reexamined the case in an article for *Skeptical Inquirer*. McGaha reported that the pattern of the lights was the same as that of a KC-97 refueling plane, which refuels other planes while both crafts are airborne. Other details of the UFO sighting, as well as a scheduled Air Force training exercise from September 2 to 3, 1965, make a compelling case for the Exeter incident being nothing more than an unusual-looking pit stop for known aircraft.

CHAPTER TWO

CLASSIC CASES

Another association many people have with UFOs has to do with the kinds of people who report sightings. People tend to think those who have encountered something inexplicable just don't have much knowledge of or experience with different aircraft, so they are not credible sources for interpreting what they've seen. However, there are plenty of UFO accounts involving experienced pilots and astronomers.

AN ICE CREAM CONE?

Captain Thomas Mantell was an experienced pilot who flew with the Kentucky Air National Guard 165th Fighter Squadron. His plane, an F-51 Mustang, was propeller driven, with a top speed of 437 mph (703 kph) and a ceiling of 41,900 feet (12,771 m), which could only be reached if the plane carried oxygen.

At about 1:20 p.m. on January 7, 1948, the Kentucky State Police reported to the Fort Knox base that "an unusual aircraft or object . . . circular in appearance, approximately 250–300 feet [76–91 m] in diameter" had been seen over Mansville, Kentucky. Fort Knox alerted

Godman Airforce Base (AFB), which sighted the object at 1:45 p.m. It looked roughly like a parachute with a red light at the bottom and was whiter than the clouds around it. It appeared to be either stationary or moving very slowly. One witness, Private First Class Stanley Oliver, said, "[T]o me it had the resemblance of an ice cream cone topped with red." It was much too large for any known balloon.

At approximately 2:40 p.m., Captain Mantell's group of four F-51s turned toward the object and began a spiral climb. At about 3:15 he reported, "I'm still climbing, the object is above and ahead of me moving at about my speed or faster. I'm trying to close in for a better look."

Somewhere between 15,000 and 22,000 feet (4,572–6,706 m), the other pilots turned back due to lack of oxygen, as they had not been traveling with extra oxygen for their low-altitude training flight. Mantell told the tower that he would go to 25,000 feet (7,620 m) for ten minutes. There followed a few garbled transmissions and then silence. Both radio and visual contact with Mantell had been lost. At 3:50 p.m., the Godman tower lost sight of the object.

Just before sunset, a number of airfield towers reported a flaming object in the midwestern sky, where it was visible for twenty minutes and then sank below the horizon. A little after 5:00 p.m., the shattered remains of Captain Mantell's F-51 were found on a farm in Franklin, Kentucky. The Captain's watch had stopped at 3:18, probably the time when his plane struck the earth.

There have been a lot of dramatic stories about Captain Mantell: that his body was missing from the crashed

Skyhook balloons were developed for atmospheric research in the late 1940s. They collected constant-level observations at very high altitudes, allowing scientists access to data they could not collect before.

plane, or that he bore strange wounds. According to records, neither claim is true. The simple truth appears to be that his curiosity got the better of him and he climbed so high that he blacked out from lack of oxygen, and his plane went into a spin and crashed. The Air Force reported that Captain Mantell had been chasing a combination of the planet Venus and two balloons and then closed the case.

In 1952, an investigator for Project Blue Book, the Air Force's famous study of UFOs, reopened the Mantell case. The investigator, Captain Edward J. Ruppelt, knew about the Navy's high-altitude research, classified in 1948, that used the huge Skyhook balloons. These balloons are 100 feet (30 m) tall and 70 feet (21 m) in diameter—as large as a small apartment building. He tried to find a launch date that might have put one of the balloons in the vicinity of Mantell's flight, but he could not verify that a Skyhook balloon had been released that day. As for Venus, while it had been seen in the daytime on that particular day, it could hardly be described as "enormous." What could have compelled an experienced pilot to ignore the dangers of oxygen deprivation and pursue this UFO to his death?

DOGFIGHT OVER FARGO

At around 9:00 p.m. on October 1, 1948, George F. Gorman of the North Dakota Air National Guard claimed to have an actual "dogfight" with a UFO. The air was clear and there was no moon. His speed was 270 miles per hour (435 kph) at an altitude of 1,500 feet (457 m). Below him he could see a Piper Cub plane circling a football field.

Then he noticed a blinking light moving swiftly from east to west. He contacted the air base's tower to see if there were other aircraft nearby. The answer was no. The pilot of the Piper Cub confirmed he could see both Gorman's F-51 Mustang and the blinking light. Gorman sped off to investigate. He pursued the object, attempting to cut it off and intending to confront it head-on, but the UFO was traveling too fast and maneuvered away from Gorman at every turn.

For a moment the lieutenant lost sight of the object, only to find it had made a turn and was heading straight for him. Suddenly it began to climb. He pushed after it, but at 14,000 feet (4,267 m) his plane stalled out. He recovered and again began circling toward the light. It pulled away and again headed straight toward him. He managed to get above the object at 14,000 feet (4,267 m) and went to full power, hoping to catch it as he dove. The light began to climb as though it would make another head-on pass, but instead went vertical and continued to climb until it was out of sight.

A man checks his hands for radioactive particles using a Geiger counter in 1947. Workers had to check their hands and feet before leaving active areas to ensure they were not contaminated.

Gorman's F-51 was checked with a Geiger counter and the reading showed measurably more radioactivity than nearby planes that hadn't been flown. Further investigation ruled out other aircraft or weather balloons in the area. This radioactivity seemed to be the first real evidence of an encounter with a flying saucer.

But then the case began to fall apart. The radioactivity was found to be typical for an aircraft flying at over 20,000 feet (6,096 m), where the thinner atmosphere offers less protection from cosmic rays that show up as increased radioactivity. In fact, a lighted weather balloon was in the area at the time of the "dogfight." The fancy flying the light seemed to be performing was an illusion caused by its movement, Gorman's own enthusiastic flying, and the lack of a reference point in the night sky. Furthermore, the witnesses in the Piper Cub didn't describe the light moving in the way Gorman said it did.

In 1949, Sidney Shalett, a writer with the *Saturday Evening Post*, asked a pilot to make several passes at a weather balloon to see if it would appear to be a highly maneuverable, pilot-operated flying saucer. The pilot flew around the weather balloon as instructed, and returned to Shalett puzzled. Shalett reported, "He came down and told me, with some surprise, it definitely appeared to be turning at the same rate as his plane, and at times it even seemed to be turning faster than his aircraft."

All of this would seem to completely discredit Second Lieutenant Gorman's experience.

Except Gorman had never claimed to fly to 20,000 feet (6,096 m).

SEARCHING EVER HIGHER

Clyde Tombaugh was an American astronomer who famously discovered Pluto at the edge of the solar system in 1930. Tombaugh built his own telescopes and cataloged more than 30,000 celestial objects, and in 2015 *The Telegraph* reported that in honor of his work and legacy, his ashes would be the first to leave the solar system aboard the NASA spacecraft *New Horizons*. With Tombaugh's credentials, he was a rare example of someone who could form one of the most informed opinions on UFO phenomena in the world.

On August 20, 1949, Tombaugh saw several UFOs near Las Cruces, New Mexico. There were six to eight rectangular lights. They were not any kind of reflection that Tombaugh

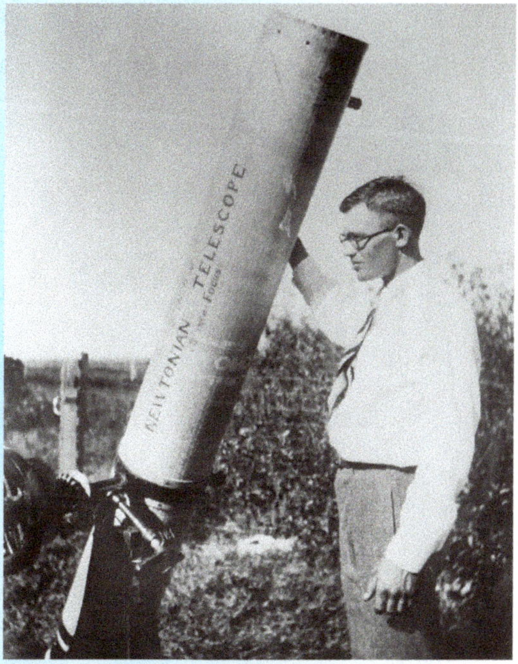

Clyde Tombaugh was only twenty-four years old when he discovered Pluto. He built several telescopes with mirrors and lenses, including the Newtonian reflecting telescope he is standing with in this photograph.

(continued on the next page)

(continued from the previous page)

had ever seen, and he was completely astonished. Over the next couple of years, Tombaugh took note of other UFOs he could not explain, including green fireballs and even an object that was four times as bright as the planet Venus at its brightest point. Tombaugh's sightings ceased after 1952 or so, but the objects he reported have left a legacy of speculation as bewildering as Tombaugh's career was extraordinary.

THE KINROSS AIR FORCE BASE INCIDENT

Also known as the Kinross Disappearance, this incident is named after the Air Force base from which Lieutenant Felix Moncla Jr.'s F-89 jet interceptor scrambled. On November 23, 1953, Truax AFB picked up a radar blip in a restricted airspace. As a precaution, Moncla and his radar officer R. R. Wilson were sent to investigate.

The object had been holding still, but suddenly it flashed off across Lake Superior while remaining visible on ground radar. Lieutenant Moncla raced after the object at over 500 mph (805 kph). After nine minutes, the F-89 began to gain slightly on the object. Ground radar operators watched as the jet closed in on the unidentified blip, until the blips suddenly seemed to merge into one.

The operators assumed that Moncla had flown over or under the UFO, but the single blip simply stayed there for a moment, then flashed off the screen. All efforts to contact Moncla by radio failed. Search and rescue crews combed the area for hours and were even aided by the Canadian Air Force. They found nothing: no trace of wreckage, no oil slick, no bodies. The *Chicago Tribune* stated that the radar operator claimed the plane had hit something, but the US Air Force quickly denied this. After suggesting that the F-89 might have hit a

The Northrop F-89 model interceptor was also known as a Scorpion because of the shape of the jet's raised tail.

Canadian DC-3 or an RCAF jet, the Canadian Air Force denied that any of its aircraft were over the lake during the chase. It's possible that the F-89 dropped into the lake without breaking up, in which case the usual signs of a crash wouldn't be apparent. That doesn't explain why radio contact ceased or why Moncla and Wilson didn't eject. And there have been numerous reports of radio transmissions being interfered with and automobile engines being stopped by UFOs.

Shortly after this incident, two fighter pilots reported that they were being followed by a UFO. Before signaling the base, they went through a series of maneuvers to make sure they weren't seeing a reflection on their canopies or perhaps an unusually bright planet. But the large, bright object stayed in the same position and continued following them. After what had happened to Moncla, they were understandably reluctant to turn in pursuit. Finally, as they neared the base, the pilots decided to make their move and turned toward the UFO. For a split second it continued to follow, then flashed off at high speed. In both cases the pursued object was never satisfactorily identified.

CHAPTER THREE

WHEN WORLDS COLLIDE

Seeing strange objects and mysterious lights in the sky is one thing, but what about the reports of UFOs that have landed on Earth? There have been accounts of everything from crop circles and bizarre metals to a space acorn and the most famous UFO incident of all—Roswell.

WRECKAGE AT THE RANCH

In December 1950, a woman visiting a dude ranch in Texas wrote to her husband about a most unusual incident. She and the other guests and ranch workers had observed what seemed to be an airplane in distress flying overhead. They thought it might have come down over the Mexican-American border. The next day several of the ranch cowboys rode out to see if they could find something. They found wreckage, but it didn't look like any airplane they'd ever seen. There were bodies strewn about, badly burned. The cowboys said it looked as though the craft had been piloted by children.

The next day they returned to find the area swarming with Mexican and American officials and military personnel arguing over jurisdiction. No one could agree if the crash remains came from north or south of the border. The cowboys were chased off before they could get too close.

The incident was described in a briefing paper for President Dwight Eisenhower. Nothing more is known about it.

OUT-OF-THIS-WORLD METAL

In September 1957, several Brazilian fishermen claimed they had seen a flying disc. It came toward them at a very high speed, dived at them, turned in a tight circle, and began a rapid climb. Seconds later it exploded, showering the beach at Ubatuba with fragments. The men wrote to the local newspaper and included several of the fragments with their letter.

When Dr. Olavo Fontes, the Brazilian representative for the Aerial Phenomena Research Organization (APRO), first read the story, he thought it must be a hoax. But he had the samples of the metal examined by a local chemist. The chemist concluded it wasn't from a meteorite because it was too light. Many meteors are composed of nickel and iron. But the samples were metal and had been burned. Spectroscopic analysis revealed the sample was magnesium and of a purity unobtainable in nature. Dr. Fontes sent a report and the samples to APRO headquarters in the United States.

THE CROP CIRCLE PHENOMENON

There have been photographs of UFOs—most proven to be fakes—and the word of people claiming to have seen strange things in the sky. But many skeptics ask what hard evidence do we actually have? And in response, many believers would point to the crop circle phenomenon.

Crop circles are strange patterns created by the flattening of crops, such as wheat, barley, or rye.

Many crop circles have been formed by hoaxers who use nearby roads and well-worn tractor paths to cover their tracks in the fields.

(continued on the next page)

(continued from the previous page)

Sometimes the patterns are extremely elaborate, and all of them can be better viewed from above. But how did they get there? No one knows when the first crop circle appeared. It may have been before cameras were invented or before it was even possible to fly over a field and notice a strange pattern. Many crop circles frequently appear near ancient artifacts, most famously near Stonehenge in southern England.

Experts noticed a rise in reports of crop circles in the 1970s, but was it because there were more crop circles or because people finally began to take notice? There is a wealth of resources on the internet showing interested pranksters how they can make their own crop circles using some rope and pieces of wood. But the idea had to come from someplace. Were crop circles invented by humans, or perhaps by extraterrestrial beings?

APRO sent a small piece of the metal to the Air Force for analysis. Unfortunately, their spectrograph operator destroyed the sample without getting an exposed plate. It may have been carelessness or a malfunction, but the destruction of the sample isn't necessarily proof of malice on the part of the Air Force. APRO then sent a sample to the Atomic Energy Commission, which found the sample was slightly denser than normal. Lab results also showed the metal probably came from something that had broken apart rapidly, as in an explosion.

Magnesium is an alkaline earth metal. It is the most lightweight structural metal and is often used in alloys for weight reduction. Magnesium is also highly reactive and produces a bright white light when ignited.

Subsequent analysis by Dr. R. S. Busk of the Condon, Colorado, UFO study revealed a high content of strontium, a soft, silver-white element. The study also said that magnesium of the same purity was created at Dow Laboratories.

It was also found that the Ubatuba samples had better high-temperature properties than samples of the Dow Labs metal. Therefore, although Dow had magnesium of equal purity, it could not have produced the samples from Brazil. How something only available in an American laboratory came to be found on a beach in Brazil was not something the Condon, Colorado, UFO study commented on.

THE FAME OF ROSWELL

On July 2, 1947, many people in Roswell reported a large, disc-shaped object flashing by overhead and showing signs of instability in its flight. An explosion was heard, but because there was a thunderstorm in progress, no particular attention was paid to the burst of sound.

The next morning, objects that were described as everything from scattered debris to "a crashed airplane without wings" or "narrow wings" and "a fat fuselage" were found.

Rancher William "Mac" Brazel found debris scattered over an area nearly 1 mile (1.6 km) long and half a mile (.8 km) wide. He collected some of it and stored it in his barn. Brazel called the sheriff when he heard about the UFO sighting, and soon news about the debris made its way to Major Jesse Marcel at the Roswell Army Air Field.

Marcel visited Brazel's place and collected some samples. Upon Marcel's return to the base, Colonel William Blanchard ordered Lieutenant William Haut to release a statement to the media that the wreckage of a flying disc had been recovered. Almost immediately, Blanchard's commanders ordered that the story be retracted.

Warrant Officer Irving Newton was an experienced weather forecaster who was called to identify some of the debris found at the Roswell UFO site. He concluded that the material had come from a weather balloon.

According to Marcel, the samples he recovered included a metal that couldn't be burned but was as light as balsa wood. Some of it appeared to be struts or beams that had hieroglyphic-like writing on them. Hammering on the metal with a hammer produced no dents. There was also a type of foil-like metal that could be crumpled into a ball and then would straighten itself out.

As well-known as the Roswell crash is for the unique properties of the debris, it's better known for the five alien bodies allegedly found at the site. The bodies were clothed in flight suits without visible fasteners. Each was 5 feet (1.5 m) tall or less, thin and pale, with a head slightly larger than a human's would be, and completely hairless. The aliens' eyes were only slightly larger than those of normal humans and had pupils. Their noses were small but defined and their mouths were lipless. Their hands had four long, thin fingers.

Immediately after the crash, the debris and alleged bodies were spirited away by the Army Air Force (as it was known in 1947) and never seen again.

In 1994 and 1997, the Air Force released reports to the press regarding the Roswell incident claiming that a balloon research project code named Mogul had crashed in the area. They explained the bodies were test dummies born aloft for scientific testing. The Army Air Force units that gathered the material were simply on-site for a normal retrieval.

The Air Force claimed that a number of different incidents, often separated by years, "have been consolidated and represented to have taken place in two or three days in July 1947." This may be true, but their test dummies, while hairless, have very prominent noses and lips and look much more like puppets than anything that might once have been alive. Ufologists and other enthusiasts continue to discuss inconsistencies in the Air Force press releases, visit Roswell, and form theories about what really happened on that day in July so many decades ago.

SPACE ACORN IN PENNSYLVANIA

The Kecksburg UFO incident occurred in Pennsylvania on December 9, 1965. Thousands of people across Ontario, Canada and at least six US states reported seeing a fireball flying brilliantly through the skies, presumably a meteor that dropped hot, metallic debris over northern Ohio and Michigan. Some grass fires were ignited and there were sonic booms around Pittsburgh, Pennsylvania. About 30 miles (48.28 km) southeast in Kecksburg, residents claimed something had crashed in the woods.

A bulky replica of the Space Acorn was created for an episode of *Unsolved Mysteries* in 1990. The prop was left behind, and Kecksburg put it on display for the fortieth anniversary of the incident in 2005.

Reports on what followed vary, with residents claiming military personnel came and claimed the object and removed it on a flatbed truck, and military personnel claiming they searched the woods and found nothing. Those who allegedly saw the object said it was metal, about the size of a Volkswagen Beetle model car, and in the shape of an acorn, with strange writing around its base that resembled hieroglyphics.

The incident remained a mystery for fifty years, but in 2015, two researchers in Westmoreland County theorized that the UFO was a General Electric Mark 2 reentry vehicle intended to be a spy satellite for the Air Force. Others had speculated the satellite had been launched by Russia instead, as the incident occurred during the Cold War period. The researchers admitted that while the details they studied were compelling, their theories could not be accepted unless confirmed by NASA or another space program. As for NASA itself, it's difficult to say how much they know or how involved they were in the incident to begin with—between a lawsuit compelling them to investigate the incident more closely, stories of them believing the UFO had been a Kosmos 96 Soviet satellite, and missing boxes of files regarding the whole situation, there is no clear answer.

CHAPTER FOUR

DISTINCTLY STRANGE SETTINGS

Even astronauts have seen objects they couldn't identify during their flights in space. Strange incidents such as the Kecksburg space acorn aside, NASA generally knows what man-made objects are orbiting the earth at any given time. They keep track of satellites, discarded boosters, and other space debris. So when an astronaut in orbit contacts home about something they can't identify, NASA can usually give a definitive answer. Sometimes, however, they can't.

COMPANY IN THE VOID

Astronaut James McDivitt on *Gemini IV* in 1965 spied a silvery-white cylindrical object with arms or antennae projecting from it. It appeared to be moving toward him when suddenly it disappeared.

During an air-to-ground transmission, McDivitt was asked, "You still looking at that thing up there?" The astronaut answered, "No, I've lost it . . . I only had it for just a minute. I got a couple of pictures . . . but I was in free drift, and before I could get the control back I drifted and lost it."

On the third day of *Gemini V*, an eight-day mission flown by LeRoy Gordon Cooper and Charles Conrad in August 1965, Flight Director D. Christopher Kraft asked, "Hey, do you guys have anything flying alongside of you?"

The astronauts replied, "Negative. Why did you ask?"

"We have a radar image of a space object going right along with you from two thousand to ten thousand yards (1,829–9,144 m) away," Flight Director Kraft said. "Their radar return is approximately the same magnitude as *Gemini V*."

Cooper and Conrad still denied seeing anything.

In the log is the following statement: "A tumbling radar signature was observed. This info is to be withheld pending further investigation."

Cape Canaveral continued to track the UFO until *Gemini V* dropped below the curve of the earth. When *Gemini V* reached the next tracking station in Carnarvon, Australia, the UFO was gone.

In 1965, *Gemini VII* astronauts Frank Borman and James Lowell contacted Houston to say they had "a bogey at twelve o'clock high." Ground control thought at first that it was the booster from their own rocket, but the astronauts said they had that in sight at the same time as they were watching the UFO. It slowly tumbled out of sight and still remains unidentified.

Michael Collins and John W. Young in *Gemini X* observed five objects in orbit together. These, too, could not be identified.

On their way to the first moon landing in 1969, the *Apollo XI* crew—Aldrin, Armstrong, and Collins—were one day out when they saw something strange. Thinking they were looking at their own Saturn IV booster rocket, they called Houston for confirmation only to be told the booster was 6,000 miles (9,656 km) away.

The UFO seemed to the astronauts to be of "a sizeable dimension" and appeared brighter than other objects going by. Armstrong said during the mission debriefing, "We should say it was right at the limit of the resolution of the eye. It was very difficult to tell just what shape it was. And there was no way to tell the size without knowing the range [distance from the *Apollo XI*] or the range without knowing the size."

At one angle, the object had a shape something like "an open suitcase." When looked at through an off-focus sextant it appeared "to be a hollow cylinder" or "two rings." When they changed the focus on the sextant, the cylinder was replaced by "this open book shape." The object remains unidentified.

The crew of Skylab II in 1973 also sighted something mysterious in space. It seemed to be a large, star-shaped object, but brighter than a planet or a star. The crew watched it slowly rotate for about ten minutes, estimating that it was between 30 and 50 nautical miles (56–93 km) from Skylab. Despite the best efforts of NASA and the North American Air Defense Command, it, too, remains unidentified.

In 2005, US astronaut Leroy Chiao was commander of the International Space Station (ISS) for six and a half months. He was performing a spacewalk outside the

Dr. Leroy Chiao spent more than thirty-six hours doing spacewalks, or Extra-Vehicular Activity (EVA), during his more than 229 days in space.

ISS when he saw lights fly by in a single line that resembled a check mark, only upside down. Some speculated that he had seen the lights of a fishing boat hundreds of miles below him on Earth, but Chiao was not sure what he saw. He revisited the incident in an interview with *NASA's Unexplained Files* in 2014, saying that while he's skeptical humanity has been visited by alien life, he

SPACE JUNK

Ever see an unexplained glowing object in the sky and think it was a UFO? There might be a simple explanation that would have made no sense a hundred years ago. Ever since humans have begun to explore space, they've been leaving traces of their travels behind. There are spent rocket stages, dead satellites, and fragments from explosions and collisions all left by space expeditions traveling in orbit around the earth.

If a piece of "space junk" breaks through the atmosphere and falls to Earth, the velocity at which it travels would cause it to burn up, emitting a glow. Could many sightings over the last century be caused by space debris?

keeps an open mind and does believe there's other life in the universe.

RENDLESHAM FOREST INCIDENT

While the United States has Roswell, the United Kingdom has Rendlesham Forest. In late 1980, a number of strange sightings of unexplained lights were reported near Rendlesham Forest in Suffolk, England. Two NATO air bases, RAF Bentwaters and RAF Woodbridge, are

The UK Forestry Commission offers a leaflet for decoding "alien symbols" along the Rendlesham Forest UFO trail. Following the path, visitors will also find a replica of what the 1980 UFO is believed to have looked like.

situated near the forest, and they were both being leased to the US Air Force at the time, so witnesses to the strange events that occurred included military personnel and security police.

Ground traces, radioactive anomalies, and a strange, glowing metal object were all reported. The craft of unknown origin emitted a bright white light that illuminated the entire forest. Theories of what caused the phenomena range from a downed Soviet spy satellite to activity at the air bases to a plain old hoax.

BEAM ME UP

In the mountains of Washington State, fourteen forestry workers were planting seedling trees when three of them noticed a small, disc-shaped object drifting over a nearby ridge. At first the three thought it might be a parachute, but they quickly realized it wasn't. It silently descended into a valley north of them with a slight "wobble" to its flight, traveling toward a herd of elk. It succeeded in getting quite close to the animals before the elk bolted. Most of them ran up a slope to the east to escape the object.

One adult, however, trotted north. The object quickly moved directly above the lone elk and lifted it off the ground, though the watching men couldn't see how this was done.

The object seemed to wobble more. As it rose higher, the elk that was suspended below the disc rotated slowly beneath it and seemed to be pulled closer to it. The witnesses said that the object seemed to grow slightly after it had picked up the animal.

The elk is one of the largest species of deer. They grow to be between 4 and 5 feet (1.2–1.5 m) tall, and a male's antlers can grow up to 4 feet above its head in addition to that!

DEBUNK IT!

Spending time on YouTube, viewers will likely encounter many videos of alleged of alien sightings and UFOs. With computer technology or the right prop or costume, almost anyone can fake a video of a sighting. How can one distinguish a real sighting from a clever fake?

- Check news sites around the area of the sighting for confirmation that it was genuine. If there are no results, it was probably fake.
- Submit articles found online to Snopes.com. The fact-finding website specializes in separating hoaxes and urban legends from reality.
- Keep in mind most sightings are unconfirmed. It's usually best to assume a video is fake until proven otherwise.

As much as people want the reassurance of "seeing is believing," video editing has become so advanced that deceiving anyone who doesn't know about such tricks can be easy for an editing pro.

With the elk below it, the object slowly ascended the slope toward some trees. It seemed to brush the tops of the trees and then reverse. Making a 360-degree turn, which resulted in greater altitude, it headed toward the trees again, moving more quickly and at a steeper angle.

As it climbed higher, the men could no longer see the elk, and they assumed that it must have been brought into the craft, although they hadn't seen any sort of door through which it might have entered. The object continued to ascend and simply disappeared from sight.

Afterward, the witnesses said the herd of elk remained in the general area but more closely huddled together than they had been. One of the witnesses added, "And so were we."

If their account is true, what happened to the elk if it was in fact taken aboard an alien spacecraft? Some conspiracy theorists may argue the extraterrestrials are trying to learn more about life on Earth by studying its strange creatures. This would not be the first supposed alien abduction. And it likely won't be the last.

CHAPTER FIVE

UFOS IN POP CULTURE AND BEYOND

While there are many baffling real-life UFO incidents to keep people's interest, there are even more options to explore for those who just want to enjoy the possibilities that fictional UFO stories entertain. There are plenty of examples in science fiction that have spurred science in the real world too, and the more ideas available to budding scientists, the better the chances that humanity will continue to learn and grow.

DON'T TOUCH THAT DIAL

One of the most famous UFO incidents known to popular culture was Orson Welles's 1938 radio drama of the H. G. Wells science fiction story, *The War of the Worlds*. As the legend goes, Orson Welles and his fellow castmates performed the story as if it were a real radio news broadcast, provoking mass hysteria as millions of Americans believed they were being invaded by aliens. It's a fascinating case study in how media, deception, and the unknown can all affect the masses—that is, if it's true. As a 2013 article in Slate revealed, it's more likely that newspapers had exaggerated the fallout from Welles's broadcast, as radio news was damaging newspaper sales and print publications may have tried to damage the reputation of radio as a medium by playing up its supposed dangers.

Nevertheless, *The War of the Worlds* has maintained its popularity over the last century. In 1996, movie audiences saw the reinvention of the story with the box office smash *Independence Day*. Rather than actual viruses, in *Independence Day* the invaders were instead thwarted by computer viruses. And 2005 brought with it Steven Spielberg's *War of the Worlds*, starring Tom Cruise and Dakota Fanning. The novel is over one hundred years old, but the very real idea of invaders from space is an idea that maintains its popularity.

BROADENING HORIZONS

But what if, unlike *The War of the Worlds*, UFOs aren't bringing extraterrestrials to Earth for malevolent purposes, but to study humans and communicate?

The 1977 film *Close Encounters of the Third Kind* asked that very question. Mysterious lights in the sky begin to appear. Roy Neary, played by Richard Dreyfuss, is one of the first to witness them. He begins to find himself drawn to the aliens, eventually bringing him to Devil's Tower in Wyoming, and he soon discovers that the aliens are not there to harm humans, only to learn more about them and communicate. What begins as a

World UFO Day began in 2001. It occurs on July 2 each year, in honor of the anniversary of the Roswell UFO incident.

terrifying encounter with mysterious lights in the sky ends with a touching first contact with beings from another planet.

Friendly extraterrestrials also appear in the films *Cocoon* (1985), *E.T.: The Extra-Terrestrial* (1982), and in the animated film *Lilo & Stitch* (2002).

In the 2006 graphic novel *Cowboys & Aliens*, creator Scott Mitchell Rosenberg takes a different approach. When a spaceship arrives in the Wild West to take over Earth, what they don't count on is a group of cowboys standing in their way. A movie based on the graphic novel, starring Daniel Craig, Harrison Ford, and Sam Rockwell, was released in 2011.

Enthusiasm abounds for UFOs. Many people remain optimistic about contact with alien life, regardless of horror movies or blockbuster adventures of alien invasion. They encourage awareness of UFOs from outer space with efforts like World UFO Day, a day for people to gather together and watch the skies. One of the goals of holding such an annual holiday is to encourage governments to declassify their records regarding UFOs, too.

A DIFFERENT KIND OF HOLLYWOOD ENCOUNTER

Late 2017 saw a particular surge in public attention to UFO phenomena and the question of whether or not extraterrestrial life is real and visiting planet Earth. In one instance, Mexican filmmaker Guillermo del Toro shared his own encounter with a flying saucer.

Del Toro and his friend were spending time talking and stargazing in a mountainous area of Mexico when they saw a light on the horizon moving at an impressive speed. They were the only ones by the roadside at the time, and del Toro and his friend began honking the horn and flashing the lights of their vehicle at the erratic light in the distance. The UFO seemed to flash instantly closer to the pair, and del Toro turned the car around to drive away from it. At first glance, it seemed to be following them, but once del Toro checked again, it was gone.

Though the encounter itself was thrilling, del Toro, who's known for his fantastical stories and captivating art style, expressed disappointment with what they had seen. Of the UFO itself, *Newsweek* reported del Toro said, "It was a flying saucer. So clichéd....It's so sad. I wish I could reveal they're not what you think they are. They are what you think they are. And the fear we felt was so primal."

GOVERNMENT ADMISSIONS

Speaking of governments declassifying their records regarding UFOs, in December 2017, the *New York Times* published an article regarding a mysterious UFO program the Pentagon had supposedly cancelled in 2012. The program was called the Advanced Aerospace Threat Identification Program, and had supposedly been operating from 2007 until 2012. However, Pentagon officials acknowledged that the program lived on and, according to Luis Elizondo, then head of the program,

After leaving his government position, Luis Elizondo began work at To The Stars Academy, an organization that seeks to reveal break-through scientific research without bureaucratic restrictions.

the only thing that had ended was the government funding for the program.

Elizondo resigned in October 2017, protesting "what he characterized as excessive secrecy and internal opposition." In his resignation letter, Elizondo expressed belief in the value of the program, asking Defense Secretary Jim Mattis why more time and resources were not being directed toward the issue. He declined to name who was succeeding him as head of the program.

TIPS FOR CLOSE ENCOUNTERS

What should someone do if they see a UFO? The same thing they should do if they witness an accident.

1. Remain calm. Getting too excited can make someone forget important details.
2. Notice things: the time the object was first seen, when it disappeared, what direction the object came from, and where it went. Were there airplanes in the sky at the same time? If so, where were they in relation to the object and what were they doing (for example, were they chasing it)?
3. Take pictures if there's a camera availalbe. If at all possible, witnesses should try to include something that will give an idea of the object's size, such as a tree or telephone pole.
4. Write down the encounter. This is where a witness's attention to details, such as the time and the direction of the object's flight, will come in

handy. A diagram of the flight path, including any zigzagging it made, as well as a drawing of the object itself, will be helpful.

5. If there are multiple witnesses, they should not discuss what they've seen until everyone has written about it and made their own drawings. Witnesses almost always see things differently, and when they discuss the event, they may change each other's memory of what they've witnessed.
6. If the UFO has left physical evidence, such as

Known objects in the foreground and background of a photograph provide a reference point for the size of any UFO being recorded.

pieces of metal or even footprints, they should not be touched. They should be left as they are, perhaps placing a marker beside the evidence to make it easier to find again.

7. VERY IMPORTANT. Witnesses should not approach the UFO if it should land or come close to the earth. There have been reports of people suffering burns or developing strange, warty growths over their exposed skin.
8. Report the sighting as soon as possible. Witnesses can contact one of the following:

    - UFO Reporting and Information Service:
      call (206) 721-5035
    - Mutual UFO Network:
      call (888) 817-2220 or visit http://www.mufon.com/report-a-ufo.html
    - National UFO Reporting Center:
      call (206) 722-3000 or visit http://www.ufocenter.com/reportform.html

Even though many UFOs turn out to be nothing more than celebratory balloons, weather instruments, or space debris, the truth can only be found if people continue to record their observations and share them with the world.

GLOSSARY

airborne Currently in the air.

briefing paper A short statement or summary of important facts.

ceiling The maximum altitude a given aircraft can reach.

connotation An implied association with something.

debriefing To be asked questions about a completed mission or undertaking.

debris Scattered fragments, especially of wreckage.

diagram A drawing meant to represent an object or area showing the relation between parts or places.

disc A flat, thin circular object.

dogfight Close combat between fighter aircraft.

extraterrestrial Outside the earth or its atmosphere. An alien being.

fallout Negative consequences.

hieroglyphic Words written in the form of pictures instead of letters.

interceptor A small jet aircraft designed to catch and fight other planes.

magnitude A thing's size or extent. In astronomy, it refers to the relative brightness of a star, ranging from a rating of one for the brightest to six for those just visible to the naked eye.

maneuverable Capable of quick and light or skillful movement.

metallic Metal-like in appearance.

meteor Any particle of matter that can be observed by its heat and glow upon entering the atmosphere.

nautical mile A unit of approximately 2,025 yards (1,852 meters).

reference point A fixed place from which position and distance are reckoned.

sextant A navigational tool that is used to measure altitudes as well as the angular distances between objects.

spectrograph An apparatus for photographing the spectrum.

squadron A unit of ten to eighteen aircraft.

tower Referring to a control tower: a tall building at an airport from which air traffic is controlled.

transport A ship or aircraft used to carry soldiers or supplies.

ufologist Someone who studies UFO phenomena.

FOR MORE INFORMATION

Center for the Study of Extraterrestrial Intelligence (CSETI)
PO Box 4556
Largo, MD 20775
(888) 382-7384
Website: http://www.cseti.org
Twitter: @DrStevenGreer
CSETI is a nonprofit international scientific organization dedicated to investigating extraterrestrial intelligence.

Committee for Skeptical Inquiry
Box 703
Amherst, NY 14226
(716) 636-1425
Website: http://www.csicop.org
Facebook: @skepticalinquirer
Twitter: @SkeptInquiry
The mission of the Committee for Skeptical Inquiry is to promote scientific inquiry, critical investigation, and the use of reason in examining controversial and extraordinary claims.

International UFO Museum and Research Center
114 North Main Street
Roswell, NM 88203
(800) 822-3545
Website: http://www.roswellufomuseum.com
Facebook: @UFOmuseum
This museum is dedicated to the preservation of Roswell research and artifacts.

J. Allen Hynek Center for UFO Studies (CUFOS)
PO Box 31335
Chicago, IL 60631
(773) 271-3611
Website: http://www.cufos.org
CUFOS is dedicated to the continuing examination and analysis of the UFO phenomenon. They also maintain an archive of publications regarding UFOs.

Library and Archives Canada
395 Wellington Street
Otawa, ON K1A 0N4
Canada
(866) 578-7777
Website: www.bac-lac.gc.ca/eng/Pages/home.aspx
Facebook and Twitter: @LibraryArchives
Library and Archives Canada provides a database of around 9,500 digitized documents regarding sightings and investigations of UFOs across Canada.

MUFON Ontario
1395 Lawrence Avenue West
Suite 20030
Toronto, ON M6L 1A7
Canada
(905) 278-9596
Website: http://www.mufoncanada.com
Twitter: @Mufon123
MUFON Ontario maintains a sighting database and facilitates access to major research laboratories across Canada for UFO researchers.

Mutual UFO Network (MUFON)
2619 11th Street Road
Greeley, CO 80634
(888) 817-2220
Website: http://www.mufon.com
Twitter: @mufon
This organization is dedicated to investigating UFO sightings, promoting research on UFOs, and educating the public on the UFO phenomenon.

National Aviation Reporting Center on Anomalous Phenomena
235 Louisiana Street
Vallejo, CA 94590
(707) 554-0886
Website: http://www.narcap.org
Facebook: @NARCAP.org
Twitter: @NARCAP1
The National Aviation Reporting Center on Anomalous Phenomena was established in late 2000 in response to an identified need for high quality scientific and technological data about so-called anomalous aerial phenomena of various kinds and US aviation safety.

FOR FURTHER READING

Coddington, Andrew. *Aliens, UFOs, and Unexplained Encounters* (Paranormal Investigations). New York, NY: Cavendish Square Publishing, 2018.

Corso, Philip J. and William J. Birnes. *The Day After Roswell.* New York, NY: Gallery Books, 2017.

Friedman, Stanton T. *The UFO Cover-Up* (Alien Encounters). New York, NY: Rosen Publishing, 2018.

Greer, Steven M. and Steve Alten. *Unacknowledged: An Exposé of the World's Greatest Secret.* West Palm Beach, FL: A&M Publishing, L.L.C., 2017.

Hawksett, David. *Extraterrestrials: Can You Find Them in the Universe?* (Be a Space Scientist!). New York, NY: Rosen Publishing, 2018.

Loh-Hagan, Virginia. *Roswell* (Urban Legends: Don't Read Alone!). Ann Arbor, MI: Cherry Lake Publishing, 2017.

McCollum, Sean. *Handbook to UFOs, Crop Circles, and Alien Encounters.* North Mankato, MN: Capstone Press, 2017.

Prothero, Donald R. *UFOs, Chemtrails, and Aliens: What Science Says.* Bloomington, IN: Indiana University Press, 2017.

Randle, Kevin D. *Encounter in the Desert.* Wayne, NJ: New Page Books, 2018.

Redfern, Nick. *The Roswell UFO Conspiracy: Exposing a Shocking and Sinister Secret.* Bracey, VA: Lisa Hagan Books, 2017.

Redfern, Nick. *365 Days of UFOs: A Year of Alien Encounters.* Bracey, VA: Lisa Hagan Books, 2017.

Salas, Robert. *Inside the UFO Archives* (Alien Encounters). New York, NY: Rosen Publishing, 2018.

BIBLIOGRAPHY

Carey, Thomas J. *Witness to Roswell: Unmasking the Government's Biggest Cover-Up*. Pompton Plains, NJ: Career Press, 2009.

Cooper, Helene, Ralph Blumenthal, and Leslie Kean. "Glowing Auras and 'Black Money': The Pentagon's Mysterious U.F.O. Program." *The New York Times*, December 16, 2017. https://www.nytimes.com/2017/12/16/us/politics/pentagon-program-ufo-harry-reid.html.

Davenport, Peter B. "Elk Abduction in Washington State." National UFO Reporting Center,February 25, 1999. http://www.nuforc.org/CB990225.html.

Eghigian, Greg. "How UFO Reports Change with the Technology of the Times." *Smithsonian Magazine*, February 1, 2018. https://www.smithsonianmag.com/history/how-ufo-reports-change-with-technology-times-180968011.

Friedman, Stanton, T. *Flying Saucers and Science: A Scientist Investigates the Mysteries of UFOs*. Pompton Plains, NJ: Career Press, 2008.

Gill, Lauren. "UFO Spotted by Guillermo del Toro in Mexican Mountains, *Shape of Water* Director Reveals." *Newsweek*, December 25, 2017. http://www.newsweek.com/ufo-spotted-guillermo-del-toro-mexican-mountains-shape-water-director-reveals-758742.

Huffaker, Christopher. "Allegheny County Leads the State in Reports of UFOs and Bigfoot." *Pittsburgh Post-Gazette*, July 31, 2017. http://www.post-gazette.com/local/region/2017/07/31/bigfoot-ufo-paranormal-sightings-kecksburg-allegheny-county-cryptids-thunderbirds-pittsburgh/stories/201707310058.

Knapton, Sarah. "Clyde Tombaugh Ashes Will Be First to Leave Solar System." *The Telegraph*, July 14, 2015.

https://www.telegraph.co.uk/news/science/science-news/11739941/Clyde-Tombaugh-ashes-will-be-first-to-leave-solar-system.html

Majors, Dan. "Five Decades Later, the Kecksburg UFO Is Identified (Probably)." *Pittsburgh Post-Gazette*, December 6, 2015. http://www.post-gazette.com/news/science/2015/12/06/50-years-later-the-Kecksburg-Westmoreland-County-UFO-is-identified-probably/stories/201512060146.

Marcel, Jesse. *Roswell Legacy: The Untold Story of the First Military Officer at the 1947 Crash Site.* Pompton Plains, NJ: Career Press, 2008.

McGaha, James, and Joe Nickell. "'Exeter Incident' Solved! A Classic UFO Case, Forty-FiveYears 'Cold'." *Skeptical Inquirer* Volume 35.6, November/December 2011.

Schlenoff, Dan. "Aliens and Nazis and Electric History, Oh My!" *Scientific American*, September 12, 2011. https://blogs.scientificamerican.com/observations/aliens-and-nazis-and-electric-history-oh-my.

Waring, Scott C. *UFO Sightings of 2006–2009.* Bloomington, IN: iUniverse, 2010.

Watkins, Eli. "Video Shows Navy Jet's Encounter with a UFO, Group Says." CNN, March 13, 2018. https://www.cnn.com/2018/03/12/politics/unidentified-aircraft-navy/index.html.

Watkins, Eli, and Brian Todd. "Former Pentagon UFO Official: 'We May Not Be Alone'." CNN, December 19, 2017. https://www.cnn.com/2017/12/18/politics/luis-elizondo-ufo-pentagon/index.html.

INDEX

A

Advanced Aerospace Threat Identification Program, 50–51
Aerial Phenomena Research Organization (APRO), 28, 30
Air Force, 10, 15–16, 18–19, 45–46, 30, 34, 36 42
airships, 7, 9
Arnold, Kenneth, 13–14
Aurora, Texas, 7–9

B

Bertrand, Eugene, 15–16
Brazel, William "Mac," 32–33

C

Canadian Air Force, 25–26
Chiao, Leroy, 39–41
Collins, Michael, 38–39
Condon, Colorado, UFO study, 31–32
crop circles, 29–30

D

declassification, 48, 50

E

Elizondo, Luis, 50–51
elk, 42–43, 45
Exeter, New Hampshire, 15–16

F

Fargo, North Dakota, 20–22
Foo Fighters, 9–10

G

ghost planes, 9, 12
Gorman, George F., 20–22

H

hieroglyphics, 33, 35

I

interceptor, 24–25
International Space Station (ISS), 39–40

K

Kecksburg, Pennsylvania, 35–36
Kinross Air Force Base, 24–26

L

Las Cruces, New Mexico, 23–24

M

magnesium, 28, 31
Mantell, Thomas, 17–20
Maracaibo, Venezuela, 11–12
Marcel, Jesse, 32–33

meteorite, 28
Mogul project, 34
Moncla, Felix Jr., 24–26
Muscarello, Norman, 15

N

NASA, 23, 36, 37, 39–40
NATO, 41
Nickell, Joe, 16

O

Oliver, Stanley, 18

P

Pentagon, 50
Pluto, 23
Project Blue Book, 19

R

radiation poisoning, 11
RAF Bentwaters, 41
RAF Woodbridge, 41
Rainier, Mount, 13–14
Rendlesham Forest, 41–42
Roswell, New Mexico, 32–34
Ruppelt, Edward J., 20

S

Shalett, Sidney, 22
Skyhook balloons, 19–20
Skylab II, 39
space acorn, 35–36
space debris, 37, 41, 53
satellites, 36, 37, 41–42
Stonehenge, 30
strontium, 31
Sweden, 12

T

Tombaugh, Clyde, 23–24

U

Ubatuba beach, 28, 31
ufologists, 16, 34

V

videos, 44

W

War of the Worlds (film), 47
War of the Worlds, The (novel), 46–47
Washington State, 42–45
weather balloons, 7, 22, 33, 53
Welles, Orson, 46
Wells, H. G., 46
Wilson, R. R., 24, 26
World UFO Day, 48
World War I, 9
World War II, 9, 12

Y

Yakima, Washington, 13
Young, John W., 38

ABOUT THE AUTHORS

Jenna Vale is a New Jersey native who has followed paranormal stories all her life. She has visited multiple sites of paranormal phenomena, from the dusty roads of *Weird NJ* fame to the haunted vaults of Edinburgh, Scotland.

Janet I. Stirling is an author of books for children and teens.

PHOTO CREDITS

Cover Igor Zh/Shutterstock.com; pp. 1, 7, 17, 27, 37, 46 (background) sakkmesterke/Shutterstock.com; p. 3 iprostocks/Shutterstock.com; pp. 4–5 (background) Mordolff/E+/Getty Images; p. 5 Traveller Martin/Shutterstock.com; p. 8 © AP Images; p. 10 Dale O'Dell/Alamy Stock Photo; pp. 13, 33 Chronicle/Alamy Stock Photo; pp. 14, 19 © Fortean/TopFoto/The Image Works; pp. 21, 23 Bettmann/Getty Images; p. 25 PF-(aircraft)/Alamy Stock Photo; p. 29 christopher jones/Alamy Stock Photo; p. 31 SPL/Science Source; p. 35 Navy2004/Wikimedia Commons/File: SpaceA.jpg/CC BY-SA 3.0; p. 40 Space Frontiers/Archive Photos/Getty Images; p. 42 Geography Photos/Universal Images Group/Getty Images; p. 43 Mountain Light Photography/Corbis Historical/Getty Images; p. 48 Svetlana Prikhnenko/Shutterstock.com; p. 50 Justin T. Gellerson/The New York Times/Redux Pictures; p. 52 M. Cornelius/Shutterstock.com; cover, back cover, and interior pages (caution pattern) Geschaft/Shutterstock.com.

Design: Michael Moy; Editor: Megan Kellerman; Photo Researcher: Karen Huang